DOG SELFIES

CHARLIE ELLIS

SUMMERSDALE PUBLISHERS LTD
46 WEST STREET
CHICHESTER
WEST SUSSEX
PO19 1RP
UK

WWW.SUMMERSDALE.COM

PRINTED AND BOUND IN THE CZECH REPUBLIC

ISBN: 978-1-84953-645-5

SUBSTANTIAL DISCOUNTS ON BULK QUANTITIES OF SUMMERSDALE BOOKS ARE AVAILABLE TO CORPORATIONS, PROFESSIONAL ASSOCIATIONS AND OTHER ORGANISATIONS. FOR DETAILS CONTACT NICKY DOUGLAS BY TELEPHONE: +44 (0) 1243 756902, FAX: +44 (0) 1243 786300 OR EMAIL: NICKY@SUMMERSDALE.COM.

TO..

FROM..

NAME:

AGE: 2 YEARS

HOBBIES: TAKING SELFIES, KICK-STARTING THE PET SELFIE CRAZE, BEING AN INSTAGRAM STAR

#DRUNKENSELFIES
#NOREGRETS

GUYS, I DON'T KNOW... WHICH IS MY BEST ANGLE?

EAT YOUR HEART OUT MILEY!

JUST CHILLIN' ON THE HUMAN BED.

#REBEL #PROHIBITEDPILLOWS

#HELLOLADIES

JUST TAKING A BREAK FROM

~~DIGGING UP ALL THE FLOWER BEDS~~

GARDENING.

NAME: BAILEY

NICKNAME: STINKY BOY!

AGE: 9 YEARS

LIKES: CHASING BIRDS AROUND THE GARD[EN]

BIGGEST FEAR: HIS STOMACH GROWLING, BECAUS[E] DOESN'T KNOW WHAT IT IS

NAME: IGGY PUP

AGE: 7 YEARS

LIKES: FROZEN PEAS, AND WILL COME RUNNING AS SOON AS HE HEARS THE FREEZER DOOR OPEN!

#ONLINEDATINGPROFILEPIC
#ALLMYOWNTEETH

NAME: BEAR

AGE: 1 YEAR

LIKES: SMILING, ADVENTURES, PLAYING WITH CATS!

#SELFIEADDICT

NAME:	COMMISSARIO COLUMBEAU FORBES
NICKNAME:	BEAU
LIKES:	CARROTS AND ICE CREAM
QUIRKS:	WAS ONCE OFFERED A JOB MODELLING DOG WEDDING OUTFITS

LOVING SOME YOGA. JUST DOING THE DOWNWARD-FACING DOG.

#EVENWHENWEAREAPART

#WECANSHAREADOGGYBED

CAN'T DO ANYTHING WITH MY HAIR
TODAY, IT'S SO FLUFFY.

#HUMBLEBRAG

NAME:	PEPE LE PUG
AGE:	5 YEARS
LIKES:	BLUEBERRIES AND THE BEACH
DISLIKES:	BIRDS AND AEROPLANES

#SURPRISEDSELFIE

#LOVELIFE

#VAYCAY

#STAYCAY

NAME: OTTO GARSED-MILLEN

LIKES: HUMANS. SITTING ON THE HEADS OF HUMANS

DISLIKES: DOGS

QUIRKS: WEEING SITTING DOWN

#ILOVERUGS

#BFF

BEEN CHOWIN' ON THOSE TEETH-CLEANING DOGGIE BISCUITS, LOVING MY SMILE ATM.

JUST BEEN FOR THE LONGEST RUN!
#COLLAPSEDSELFIE

#WHITEDOGWASTED

#NOMAKEUPSELFIE

NAME: HENRY

AGE: 5 YEARS

LIKES: HIS SWEET PAD AND LONG WALKS IN THE SUNSHINE

DISLIKES: SQUIRRELS

NOT TO MAKE ANYONE JEL, BUT HAVING THE BEST SUNBATHING WEATHER HERE.

#HAPPYFACE

#CRAZYFACE

#WALKINGLIKEHUMANS

FORGET DUCK FACE, I'M BRINGING IN DOG FACE.

DOES THIS ANGLE MAKE MY EARS LOOK BIG?

#SUNSOUT
#TONGUESOUT

NAME: WILF

AGE: 3 YEARS

LIKES: SQUEAKY BALLS, SALMON AND ICE CREAM

DISLIKES: WATER AND ANYONE WHO WON'T THROW HIS SQUEAKY BALL FOR HIM

#SUPERSMILEY

NAME: JETHRO TULL VOM TEUFELSJOCH

AGE: 3

LIKES: CATCHING THE FRISBEE, HERDING HORSES AND COWS, SNOWBALL FIGHTS AND TAKING THE OCCASIONAL SELFIE!

NAME: BUDDY STOREY

LIKES: MUDDY PUDDLES, BIG STICKS AND TWEETING

TWITTER: @BUDDYPORTSMOUTH

#PHOTOBOMB

PHOTO CREDITS

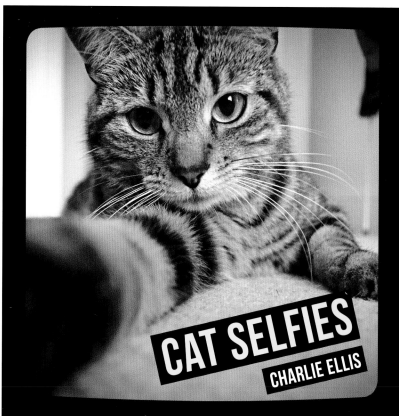

CAT SELFIES

CHARLIE ELLIS

CAT SELFIES

ISBN: 978 1 84953 646 2   HARDBACK   £6.99

EVERYONE IS SNAPPING SELFIES AND CATS ARE NO EXCEPTION! FROM THE SUBLIME TO THE RIDICULOUS, THIS BOOK COLLECTS THE BEST PHOTOS OF FELINES WHO HAVE TAKEN THE SELFIE CRAZE INTO THEIR OWN PAWS.

IF YOU'RE INTERESTED IN FINDING OUT MORE ABOUT OUR BOOKS,
FIND US ON FACEBOOK AT SUMMERSDALE PUBLISHERS
AND FOLLOW US ON TWITTER AT @SUMMERSDALE.

WWW.SUMMERSDALE.COM